The Reiki Manual

A beginner's guide to Reiki healing, how Reiki works, and why it needs to be a part of your life!

Table of Contents

Introduction

I want to thank you and congratulate you for downloading the book, *"The Reiki Manual"*.

This book contains helpful information about Reiki, what it is, and everything you need to know to get started.

Reiki is a form of alternative therapy that can be learned by anyone, regardless of educational background or status.

It is a relatively new therapy, however it has a range of different branches and styles.

Regardless of whether you want to learn how to become a Reiki teacher, or just try Reiki out, this book will provide you with the knowledge needed to begin doing so.

This book will explain to you tips and techniques that will help you successfully choose a style of Reiki to participate in, and begin implementing Reiki healing in to your life!

Thanks again for downloading this book, I hope you enjoy it!

Chapter 1: Overview of Reiki

People give high regard to health. It is considered very important by many, if not the majority of people; which is no wonder since our instincts are directed towards survival and health is a huge factor for survival.

Medical care is something that everyone is familiar with. The common procedures and medications are based on strictly scientific trials so they are widely trusted.

On the other hand is alternative medicine. While it is also popular and has its set of followers and believers, is surrounded by criticism and controversy. Not to say that conventional medical care doesn't have its own share of controversy, but it is considered more trusted than alternative medicine in western society.

Despite criticism, the practice of alternative medicine lives on. The interest is actually quite high and many organizations are opening up to the possibility that alternative medicine might actually be more effective than once thought.

Here, we will discuss about a particular practice that is classified under alternative medicine.

Reiki Healing

Reiki is an alternative healing practice from Japan. Some medical bodies classify it as oriental medicine. The term is a combined form of two words: "rei" and "ki". It can be translated to "universal life energy". Reiki is a healing discipline that makes use of a technique that is most often called "palm healing" or "laying-on of hands". The idea behind it is that, through this process, the practitioner is transferring universal energy to the patient. This universal energy, in turn, facilitates self-healing and reaching a state of equilibrium. The aim is to balance the subtle energies inside the patient's body. Reiki is believed to be able to correct imbalances in spiritual, emotional, mental, and physical aspects of the body. To perform the energy transfer, the practitioner acts as a vessel by which the healing energies go through and channeled to where the patient's body needs them the most. As the practitioner touches the patient's body, the "ki" flows through the practitioner and emanates from the palms.

There are two major branches of Reiki: the Traditional Japanese Reiki and the Western Reiki. These will be discussed further in a later chapter, but they mainly differ in that the Western version makes use of hand placements in a systematically set order while the Traditional version uses hand positions based on intuition.

Brief History

Mikao Usui, a Japanese Buddhist, first developed Reiki in 1922. Usui was in Mount Kurama participating in Isyu Guo, a Buddhist training course that lasted 21 days. The claim is that, during the Isyu Guo, Usui underwent a mystical revelation by which he gained the ability to attune other people to what he termed as Reiki. He said that this Reiki came into his body via his crown Chakra. In April of the same year, he decided to move to Tokyo and started Usui Reiki Ryoho Gakkai (translated: Usui's Spiritual Energy Therapy Method Society to spread the practice of Reiki and consequently, allow more people to receive the treatment.

Basing from Usui's memorial stone inscription, he was able to teach his Reiki system to more than 2000 people throughout his lifetime. Sixteen of them went on to attain the highest degree of training.

Usui died from a stroke in March of 1926. But he had already built a strong enough foundation for the Reiki to ensure its continuous development. J. Ushida took charge of the Gakkai, also taking responsibility over the creation and maintenance of Usui's memorial site. From then on, several more Reiki masters succeeded as the Gakkai's president.

Shortly before his death, Usui was approached by Chujiro Hayashi with a proposition for developing a simpler Reiki. Hayashi got Usui's agreement. After Usui died, Hayashi worked independently from the Gakkai and established his own clinic. Hayashi gave Reiki treatments and training that focused more on physical healing and involved more structured and simplified Reiki techniques.

The Principles

In the development of his Reiki system, Usui came up with a selection of ethical principles that are based on a summary of some works by literary artist Emperor Meiji, whom he admired. These principles or concepts later turned into the Five Reiki Precepts. They are:

- *Do not be angry.*
- *Do not worry.*
- *Be grateful.*
- *Work with diligence.*
- *Be kind to people.*

Today, Reiki practitioners commonly abide by these precepts.

Next...

You have seen an overview of Reiki and its history. In the next chapter, you will learn about its traditions.

Chapter 2: Reiki Traditions

Reiki practice today is divided into a multitude of branches. However, there are two main branches by which Reiki practices are commonly classified into. They are the Traditional Japanese Reiki and the Western Reiki.

Traditional Japanese Reiki

In general, Traditional Japanese Reiki is used for describing the very system established from the original teachings of Mikao Usui, as well as the other teachings that never left Japan. However, in the 1990s, Western teachers ventured to Japan with the objective of finding these certain teachings and found nothing. So, they began establishing schools teaching lower levels of Reiki to the Japanese. In 1993, Frank Arjava Petter, a Reiki master from Germany, began teaching Master level Reiki which prompted the Japanese to share their Traditional Reiki knowledge. From that point on, a number of traditions have sprung, including, but not limited to, the following:

- *Usui Reiki Ryoho Gakkai (Usui Reiki Healing Method Learning Society).* This is the society comprised by the masters of Reiki founded by Mikao Usui. Since no one knows how exactly the Gakkai practices today, it is only assumed that Usui's style remains today. Many years passed with this society remaining secret. But today, some teachings are being shared to the world. Though they still remain as a hermetic society nigh inaccessible.

- *Reido Reiki Gakkai (Spiritual Occurrence Spiritual Energy Society)*. This is the given name for the system based from the Ryoho Gakkai, led by one Fuminori Aoki. Aoki added upon the teaching of the Gakkai. This system uses the "Koriki" symbol, Aoki's inspiration.

- *Komyo Reiki Kai (Enlightened Spiritual Energy Meeting)*. This system takes from a school teaching Japanese Traditional Reiki. Hyakuten Inamoto established the said school. Inamoto has a Western Reiki background but his techniques are derived from the Hayashi teachings.

- *Jikiden Reiki (The Direct Teaching Spiritual Energy)*. This is the name for the original system that Dr. Hayashi taught. The founders are Mrs. Yamaguchi and Tadao Yamaguchi, her son.

The other main branch of Reiki is the Western Reiki. This system is widely attributed to Hawayo Takata. For this style, the focus is more on the healing of ailments and the measure for attunement is more formalized.

Takata was trained by Hayashi. After the training, Takata returned to Hawaii and there continued to spread Reiki. He then continued to expand Reiki further into the Western world. Takata, resulting from World War II, decided that modifying the Traditional Japanese Reiki was necessary to cater to the mentality of people in the West.

Here are some disciplines under the Western Reiki:

- *Usui Reiki Shiki Ryoho (common translation: Usui's Spiritual Energy Style of Therapy; literal translation: Usui's Spiritual Energy Style of Medical Treatment)*. This is used for the Western

Reiki system. This particular system tried as much as possible to stay close to the original techniques practiced by Hawayo Takata. Today, for one, this is taught by the Reiki Alliance with the leadership of Phyllis Lei Furumoto, the grand-daughter of Takata. Consistent with most Western Reiki systems, this system has three levels: the First Degree, Second Degree, and Teacher/Master Degree respectively. They use Takata's version of the four original symbols which were passed by Hayashi. In the United Kingdom, Usui Reiki Shiki Ryoho is the normally required qualification for anyone seeking to perform Reiki for the general population.

- *Usui/Tibetan Reiki.* This name is used for the system developed initially by Arthur Robertson, and popularized later through the efforts of William Lee Rand, aided by Diane Stein. The techniques derive from Usui Reiki as trained by Takata, using techniques from Usui Reiki Ryoho Gakkai. Rand gave a few additions, including a modified method of attunement, implementing Violet Breath. Symbols used include the four original Usui symbols plus kundalini fire and Tibetan MasterSymbols. This style also uses the position called hui yin and the microcosmic orbit. In addition, some practitioners of this style also incorporate what is called psychic surgery. This differs from other Western Reiki systems because it has four levels: the First Degree, the Second Degree, the Advanced Reiki Training (aka ART or 3A), and the Teacher/Master (aka 3B).

- *Gendai Reiki Ho (Modern Spiritual Energy Method).* This style mixes styles from both the Japanese Reiki and Western variations. Hiroshi Doi was the establisher of this particular style. His initial training was under Mieko Mitsui involving Western Reiki. Mieko Mitsui is known in the Reiki field as the Master of the "Radiance Technique". Later, in 1993, Doi became a member of the Usui Reiki Ryoho Gakkai.

Next...

Now you have been acquainted with the most general traditions of Reiki practice. In the next chapter, you will learn about how people learn the art. You will also see how you too can learn Reiki.

Chapter 3: Training for Reiki Practitioners

Learning Reiki Yourself

There are many reasons why you'd be interested in learning Reiki yourself. While receiving Reiki from a practitioner is great experience, Reiki self-care has a great deal of advantages. When you can treat yourself with Reiki, you can easily perform it even if you have a busy schedule. This is also beneficial if you have health issues that restrict you from travelling daily. You can readily do Reiki self-care every day to relieve stress, maintain your body's equilibrium, and feel better overall. You can also perform Reiki healing for your family.

Moreover, some anecdotal evidence suggests that Reiki can also benefit animals just like how it can with humans. If you want your pet to receive Reiki, you may have a hard time finding a practitioner willing to do so. If you can practice Reiki yourself, you won't have a problem if you want to give your pet Reiki.

Financially, the benefit of learning Reiki is also obvious. Compare a one-time learning fee to how much you'll pay for repeated sessions. Besides, you can also start your own Reiki healing center.

So, how do you learn Reiki? Are there any qualifications? The good thing is that anyone who wants to learn can do so, without any restriction regarding age or state of health. Actually, even children can be taught Reiki. You don't need any credentials or specific background to be accepted for training.

Probably, the foremost reason why there are no credentials or background needed is because of Reiki's simplicity. With only ten hours of face-to-face training, you can learn Reiki. This is generally done through group classes. You don't need to have any prior knowledge on healthcare or subtle bioenergy to attend the training.

To start learning Reiki, you have to find a Reiki Master/Teacher. They are the only ones qualified to teach Reiki. It might not be an easy task since only a handful of Reiki practitioners reach this level. Still, there are things you can do that will help you find a Master quickly. Simply find a Reiki center and ask who their teacher was.

If you don't know anyone, you can check out yoga studios and look at their bulletin boards. The same can be done from stores specializing in health food. You can even ask the local hospital if they have integrated alternative medicine into their services.

When you find Reiki Masters, you have to remember that Reiki is not yet standardized. So, anyone who has the title "Reiki Master" is not necessarily qualified to teach or train people. It will be important to check the Reiki Masters' background. Any Reiki Master will not hesitate to entertain this inquiry provided that they are really credible.

When you finally select the Reiki Master to train under, you will be ready to undergo training. Below are descriptions of the process by which practitioners train Reiki.

The Training

How does an aspiring Reiki practitioner train? In the Traditional Japanese Reiki, they are taught with concentration on Usui's teachings. They undergo meditation meetings every week. In such meetings, Reiki is given to them to be used in a process called Byosen-ho, where the body is given an energetic diagnosis. This is because Traditional Japanese Reiki focuses heavily on intuition and specific direction.

On the other hand, Western Reiki leans more towards whole body treatment instead of area-specific. Outside Japan, Reiki practitioner training is typically partitioned into three degrees or levels. The common system is described below.

First Degree

The first degree, sometimes termed as Shoden (a Japanese term meaning "Entry" or "Elementary teachings"), of a Reiki training course provides the trainee with the basics – elementary theories and procedures. The student undergoes several "attunement" processes facilitated by the instructor. They begin learning certain hand positions on a recipient's body, which are hand positions believed to have the most conducive effects for whole body treatment process. Once the trainee completes the first degree training, he or she becomes a practitioner who is allowed to use Reiki for treating himself/herself and others. The duration of this course varies depending on the teacher of Reiki. Some spread four sessions throughout a particular number of days, while others give two sessions over two days.

Second Degree

The second degree, sometimes termed as Okuden (a Japanese term meaning "Inner teachings"), the Reiki student begins to learn how to use symbols believed to improve the distance and intensity by which the Reiki energies can be emanated. The symbols are used to create a short-term connection between the Reiki practitioner and the intended recipient. The time and location doesn't matter. Once the connection is established, Reiki energies can be sent. The student undergoes further attunement, claimed to further enhance the practitioner's Reiki flow-through capacity and raise the effectiveness of the symbols. Once the student completes the second degree, he/she can be allowed to perform "distant healing", the process by which Reiki treatment is given to a recipient without the practitioner being physically present. The second degree is mostly attained after a 10-year period, sometimes even 20.

Master Level

Only a handful of Reiki practitioners complete the third degree of Reiki training. The last degree is known as "master training", sometimes termed Shinpiden (a Japanese term meaning "Mystery Teachings"). Once completed, the practitioner receives the title of Reiki Master. In the context of Reiki, A title of "master" does not mean the person has received spiritual enlightenment. Thus, "Master/Teacher" is used to avoid such confusion. Depending on the specific Reiki branch, the student may go through one or more processes of attunement. He or she will learn about one more symbol. Completing the Master level of training, the Reiki Master will be allowed to perform attunements and teach Reiki (all three degrees). There is a wide variation of master training duration. It can be as short as a day, or more than a year. This depends upon the school and/or the philosophy followed by the Reiki master who is conducting the training.

Reiki Masters fall under two common types: the Master Teacher and the Master Practitioner. A Master Teacher is a Reiki Master who can also teach Reiki to others. On the other hand, a Master Practitioner is a Reiki Master but does not train others.

Other Varieties

Aside from the degree-based training described above, there are many more variations in training methods for Reiki. They also differ in the completion speed and cost. This is probably due to the fact that, as of today, there is no accreditation for it. There's neither a central body nor any regulation regarding its practice as well. However, in the United Kingdom, organizations are working towards standardization of Reiki and its practices. Some examples are the Reiki Council (UK) and the UK Reiki Federation.

Online Reiki classes are available, but they are not accepted by many Reiki experts since they strongly believe that face-to-face attunement is necessary and irreplaceable.

Next...

Now you have learned about the basic teachings and training for Reiki. In the next chapter, you will learn more about the practice of Reiki.

Chapter 4: The Practice of Reiki

Western Reiki teaches that Reiki operates in combination with the so-called meridian energy lines as well as chakras, facilitated via hand positions. These positions are usually parallel with the body's seven major chakra points. From top to bottom they are: the Crown Chakra, the Third Eye Chakra, the Throat Chakra, the Heart Chakra, the Solar Plexus Chakra, the Sacral Chakra, and the Base or Root Chakra. The hand positions involve both the back and front part of the body; at times including specific body areas.

James Deacon, as well as other authors on the subject, have said that Mikao Usui only made use of five basic hand positions focusing from the head to the neck. In such a practice, Reiki would be given to the head to neck area. Then, the energy would flow to the body parts or areas which need treatment due to imbalances.

Western Reiki widely uses the basis of chakra, in contrast to the case of Traditional Japanese Reiki. Traditional Japanese Reiki gives more concentration to area-specific treatment, using techniques, like Reiji-ho and Byosen-ho, to pinpoint areas of discomfort in both the physical body and the aura.

Reiki Healing

When healing through the Usui Reiki Ryoho, no medication or instrument is used. Rather, the practitioner uses light tapping, touching, blowing, and looking. According to the German Reiki Master Frank Arjava Petter, Mikao Usui performed Reiki healing by touching the areas of discomfort, massaging them, giving them a light tap, stroking them, blowing on them, and gazing at them for around two or three minutes. Through these, he transferred energy to those areas of the body. Usui used what is commonly called palm healing, an alternative and complementary medicine technique. Sometimes referred to with the term tenohira (a Japanese term that can be translated to "the palm"), this palm healing process is believed by Reiki practitioners to transfer universal energy, in a form called "ki", by way of the palm to activate self-healing, as well as induce bodily equilibrium.

For the Whole Body

A Reiki whole body treatment usually starts with the practitioner instructing the would-be receiver to lie on his or her back, typically on a table for massage. The recipient is told to relax. For this, the recipient usually wears loose, comfortable pieces of clothing. The practitioner then proceeds to enter a meditative or calm mental state in order to prepare his mind for the session. This may take a few moments and is mostly done free of any excessive talking.

Once the practitioner is done preparing, he or she will proceed with the treatment. The practitioner places his/her hand on the receiver forming different positions. Practitioners may also perform a non-touch technique. In those cases, the practitioner's hands are positioned with a few centimeters of distance from the area of the body, sometimes for all or just some of the positions. Typically, the hands stay in one position for around three or five minutes and then the practitioner proceeds to the succeeding hand position. In general, these hand positions cover the body from around the head area, the torso (both the back and the front), to both knees, and lower exremeities. Positions involved can number from 12 up to

20. Duration of a whole body treatment may last between 45 and 90 minutes.

A lot of Western Reiki operates with a preset 12 hand positions; while others rely on intuition for guidance to detect areas that need treatment, just like the Traditional Japanese Reiki process. Sometimes, the practitioner starts with a "scan" to facilitate the detection. Guided by this intuition as well, the practitioner may stay longer or shorter for certain hand positions. Western Reiki healing sessions are considered as large-scale treatments while the Traditional Japanese Reiki leans more towards localized treatment.

The Western Reiki's 12 preset hand positions have been claimed to energize through several aspects:

- *The warmth coming from the hands energize the recipient on a physical level;*
- *The special symbols of Reiki energize the recipient on a mental level;*
- *The flowing of love through using the symbols energizes the recipient on an emotional level; and*
- *The company of a trained practitioner plus the flow of the universal energy itself energizes.*

Several reports state that a tingling or warm sensation in the area under treatment is felt by recipients, even in sessions using a no-physical-contact approach. The most common immediate effect that people notice is a combination of a general sense of wellness and state of great relaxation. Sometimes, emotional release may also happen.

Reiki healing is only claimed to activate the body's natural healing process. Thus, instantaneous cures for particular health issues are rarely reported. When a chronic condition is concerned, a sequence of treatments, involving at least three sessions spaced out between one and seven days, is often recommended. This is coupled with an ongoing regular treatment for maintenance of well-being. Intervals with the said type of treatments usually range between one and four weeks, unless the case is self-treatment which is commonly done on a daily basis.

Specified Treatment

For localized treatment, the practitioner places his or her hand on or near a specified part of the body with varying duration. This is the method normally preferred for recent injuries, with the treatment focusing around the injured area. The duration of these treatments vary widely, but it commonly lasts 20 minutes. Takata's description of localized treatment is "hands-on work", as opposed to distance healing.

Certain sicknesses are also treated by some practitioners using localized treatment, with several publications presenting correct hand positions. But there are also some practitioners who prefer using full body treatment for all chronic illnesses as they believe it has a holistic effect. There are other practitioners, though, who combine both: giving a full body treatment as the first part of a session, and then a localized treatment to different areas of the body for particular ailments.

In Usui's practice, he used distinctive hand positions when treating certain illnesses and discomfort, including nervous system disorders, respiratory conditions, digestive issues, circulatory system problems, blood and metabolic disorders, urogenital tract conditions, skin problems, childhood illnesses, women's health conditions, and contagious diseases.

Breathing Techniques

In Western Reiki, breathing is not given much attention. However, in many Japanese Reiki practices, using breath and breathing is a vital element. From Usui's practices again, there is a technique he used that is called the Joshin Kokyu-ho. The literal translation is "Goddess Breath Method" but in the context of Reiki, the translation is "breathing method for spirit cleansing". This particular technique is carried out by sitting straight, aligning the back, and then proceeding with breathing through the nose at a slow pace. The underlying belief for such practices is that the practitioner breaths in the Reiki via the crown chakra when he/she inhales. The objective is purification of the body to make it appropriate for the Reiki to flow into.

Next...

Now, you are familiar with the different practices of Reiki. In the next chapter, you will find out more of the benefits of Reiki healing.

Chapter 5: The Benefits of Reiki Healing

It was mentioned before that one of the immediately noticeable effects of Reiki is a feeling of relaxation. This is actually one of the primary benefits one can get from Reiki healing. A session of Reiki relieves stress from the energy recipient. Relieving stress and putting the body in a relaxed mode activates the body's natural healing capabilities. It also improves and maintains overall health as well. Relaxation has really good effects on the body. But of course, many other practices, like massages and spa treatments, can also provide stress relief and relaxation.

Reiki practice is based from the concept of "Life Force Energy". This energy is flowing within a person. When this flow is hampered in any way (maybe weakened, blocked, or outright disrupted), it can cause health or even emotional problems.

Many things in life can cause imbalances to the flow of this energy. These include injury, physical or emotional trauma, negative thoughts and emotions (fear, doubt, anxiety, worry, anger, and the like), unhealthy self-talk, toxins, improper nutrition, bad habits, and failed relationships. The physical, emotional, mental, and spiritual aspects of a person are affected when the imbalances occur. Reiki is aimed to heal problems in all of these aspects.

Reiki is simple and non-invasive which makes it appealing to many people. This discipline of alternative medicine provides treatments for a person suffering in a physical, emotional, mental, or spiritual sense.

There are many reported benefits of Reiki healing. But you should be aware that these are from testimonials and anecdotes. Reiki is yet to be completely scientifically proven (more on this in a later chapter). However, these benefits make Reiki worthy of attention as an alternative medicine, both from people seeking healing and the medical science community for scientific studies. Here are some of them:

- Reiki helps get a person into deep relaxation, relieving daily stress and tension.
- Reiki activates the body's natural healing capability.
- Many people who have received Reiki healing reported that they were able to sleep better.
- Reiki helps reduce blood pressure.
- Reiki has been used for treating both acute and chronic conditions.
- Reiki is reported to also help in breaking off from addictions.
- Reiki helps in relieving pain.
- Reiki is said to also help the body clean itself from accumulated toxins.
- Some people believe Reiki strengthens the immune system.
- There are claims that Reiki slows down aging and improves vitality.
- For people seeking spiritual growth, Reiki is said to be one of the best ways.

When Reiki is practiced over a long duration, the flow of the universal energy in one's body is maintained in equilibrium. Thus, the general well-being is also kept in good condition.

Next...

You have seen the list of reported benefits from Reiki healing. In the next chapter will be a discussion on some controversies regarding the credibility of Reiki.

Chapter 6: Controversies

Inconclusive?

While Reiki has a good deal of followers and practitioners, there are many who doubt it as well, similar with almost any alternative medicine.

One reason is that the very basic mechanism by which Reiki operates, which is the existence of "ki" or "life force", is still hypothetical. It has not yet been proven scientifically.

However, many organizations have shown an interest in scientifically testing Reiki. In 2008, a systematic study involving randomized clinical trials was conducted to evaluate the efficacy of Reiki. The study didn't find solid demonstrations of the effectiveness of Reiki for treating any condition. The problem is that several factors make it hard to quantify different aspects of Reiki which makes a scientific conclusion also difficult to arrive at. Most of the data simply cannot be interpreted. Most studies didn't fulfill an adequate sample size, or the design and reporting were lacking. Furthermore, the control for placebo effects proves to be really hard since, unlike a drug, designing a realistic placebo is difficult for a practice like Reiki. Thus, a quantifiable effectiveness rate is not yet established for Reiki. Its effectiveness remains inconclusive to this date.

Safety

The concern over Reiki's safety is the same as with its fellow alternative medicines. Many conventional medicine professionals are apprehensive about patients engaging in alternative therapies, preferring scientifically proven medical treatments. However, unlike some alternative medicine practices, Reiki practitioners actually encourage patients to go to a doctor when it comes to serious conditions, and just recommend Reiki as a complement, not a replacement, of conventional medicine. In clinical trials, there were no adverse effects reported from undergoing Reiki healing.

Internal Conflicts

Aside from conflicts with the scientific community, Reiki also has its share of internal controversies. This is quite expected because if the wide variety of teaching, training, and practicing styles. The two major traditions are even divided into many sub-branches. With these come different and even contradicting principles. Some branches don't agree with the very nature of the Reiki energy. Some argue about the secrecy of the symbols used. Attunement methods are also a point of argument. The conflicts within the Reiki practice do not stop with teachings and methods. For example, there are even debates surrounding the fees charged for Reiki Training.

Catholic Tension

In the United States, the Catholic Church became concerned about Reiki. They eventually prohibited Catholic Church members to practice of Reiki, particularly in Catholic hospitals and retreat centers. In the decree where this is declared, the conclusion is that Reiki would be inappropriate to be practiced by Catholics since it is not included in Christian teachings and it is not yet scientifically proven.

Well...

Reiki is not yet proven scientifically; that much is true. However, the practice remains strong and widespread to this date since it has not been disproved as well. As discussed earlier, the effects of Reiki are hard to quantify and studies are inconclusive not because of the Reiki practice itself but rather with the design of the studies. The good thing is that the benefits reported are worthwhile and Reiki is proven safe. Thus, trying it out wouldn't be problematic at all.

Conclusion

Thank you again for downloading this book!

I hope this book was able to help you learn more about Reiki.

The next step is to put this information to use, and begin practicing Reiki healing as a part of your life!

Decide on a style of Reiki that sits well with your beliefs, and sounds appropriate to you. Remember that Reiki is not a replacement for modern medicine or treatment, and is rather seen as a complementing form of treatment.

Although the benefits have not been scientifically proven, Reiki is safe to try. So, you have nothing to lose through trying for yourself!

Finally, if you enjoyed this book, please take the time to share your thoughts and post a review on Amazon. It'd be greatly appreciated!

Thank you and good luck!

www.ingramcontent.com/pod-product-compliance
Lightning Source LLC
Chambersburg PA
CBHW061107050726
47592CB00004B/1865